# Super Winter Survivors

Diane Blair and Pamela Wright

## Contents

Rigby

A Harcourt Achieve Imprint

www.Rigby.com
1-800-531-5015

# The Long Road Ahead

Every fall, the animal world begins buzzing with activity. Beavers, woodchucks, and badgers all work hard building dens and shelters. As the leaves turn orange, red, and yellow, birds of all kinds take to the air for warmer climates. The air turns crisp and cool, and bears start eating much more than usual—they want to get as fat as possible.

They do this because winter is coming.

Winter is a time of cold and a time of want. During the winter, plants and grasses are in short supply. There is very little prey for the predator. The snows bring temperatures below 0° Fahrenheit, winds that cut like a knife, and a world buried in white.

As the autumn leaves turn, the animal kingdom senses the change of the seasons. It's time to make preparations for the wintry time ahead.

There's a long road ahead. If a chipmunk, or an elk, or an Arctic bird has any chance of making it, it needs a **survival strategy**. It needs a plan for living through the winter.

Soon it's January, and the animal world is quiet with the cold.

You're about to discover the survival strategies of several animal species. These animals are serious winter survivors. Some will sleep through this difficult season. Some will run, fly, or swim from it. Others will stay and **adapt**.

So grab your coat and scarf. It's time to head out into the snow!

# Chapter One

# "Wake Me in the Spring"

There's one way of making it through the cold that takes very little energy—you just sleep through it. Some animals take a really, really long nap through the winter months until spring returns with warmer weather. This is called **hibernation**.

Hibernation is more than just going to sleep for the night. In fact, a hibernating animal won't wake for weeks or months at a time. Its entire body slows down as it lowers its **metabolic rate**. The metabolic rate is a measure of:

- how fast or slow an animal breathes,
- how much body heat it generates,
- how fast it burns the food it eats,
- how fast its heart pumps blood, and
- how much energy the animal uses to live.

In winter, a little bit has to go a long way, so an animal will lower its metabolic rate so it doesn't need as much food to live.

Some bats like to hibernate alone, but most bats hibernate in groups.

Many different animal species hibernate, such as squirrels, bats, possums, hedgehogs, and spiny anteaters. Scientists have studied hibernating animals for years in hopes of learning more about how this process works. In northeastern Minnesota in the fall of 1999, scientists found the best test subject of all. They found a 3-year-old black bear named Whiteheart.

The spiny anteater's vision is weak, but it can sniff out ants and termites, which it licks up with its long, sticky tongue.

# Whiteheart the Black Bear

Black bears are one of nature's best hibernators. Their survival rate is close to 99 percent, far higher than any other species—including early humans. In fact, some American Indian tribes believed that bears were much smarter than people because they knew how to survive the long winter months.

Because bears are such good hibernators, scientists with the North American Bear Center put a radio collar on Whiteheart, their test bear. The collar kept track of what Whiteheart did, when she slept, and where she went.

They also put a Webcam inside Whiteheart's den. The camera recorded Whiteheart 24 hours a day and sent the images out live over the Internet. Elementary school classes logged in every week to watch. For the first time, the world was able to observe a black bear hibernating through the winter.

## Whiteheart Gets Ready for Bed

The first thing Whiteheart did as winter approached was to start eating lots of berries, plants, and small prey. She gained nearly 30 pounds a week in order to pack on a lot of body fat. Hibernators have two kinds of fat: white fat and brown fat. White fat is stored in the belly and is burned as energy while the animal sleeps. Brown fat clumps across the animal's shoulders, back, brain, heart, and lungs. Brown fat keeps the animal warm and protects its organs from the cold temperatures. The animal also uses it in the spring when it wakes up.

Black bears like these spend the winter sleeping in dens made out of caves, deep holes in the ground, or anywhere where they can find a roof over their heads.

Next it was time to find shelter. Whiteheart prepared a den in a shallow cave in the side of a mountain. A fallen fir tree covering the entrance gave extra protection from the snow. Whiteheart spent several weeks bringing in leaves and twigs for her bed.

Scientists noticed that she was growing a thick **pelt** of fur. This extra fur would make a nice, warm blanket against the cold. Almost all furry animals grow a winter coat for the cold weather, even household pets. When the temperature rises in the spring, they simply shed the extra fur.

In early November of 1999, Whiteheart had found the perfect den, prepared her bed, and stored enough extra fat to live on for the next several months. Fall was almost over, and so Whiteheart laid down to sleep.

# The Webcam Watches

Whiteheart's metabolic rate slowed, just as the scientists thought it would. Her temperature dropped to 88° F, which is only about 12° F below normal. This was surprising because the body temperature of other hibernators, such as the woodchuck, can drop to as low as 50° F.

The heart rate of a black bear is normally 50 beats per minute. While hibernating, Whiteheart's heart rate dropped to about 8 beats per minute. That's only once every 7 seconds!

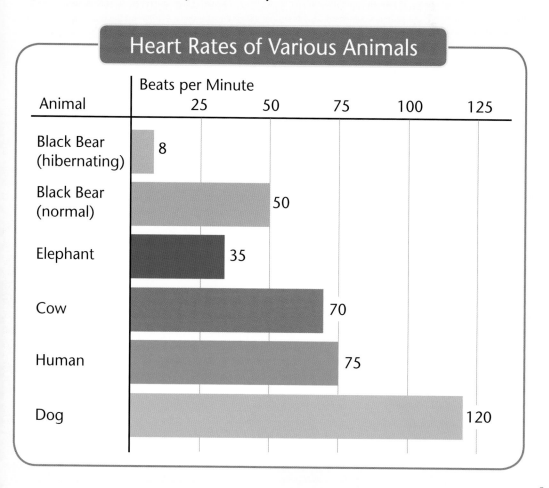

Outside the den, winter was at its worst. Throughout December and January, Whiteheart spent weeks at a time in a deep sleep. Visitors logged onto the Web site and saw the same thing day after day—a big, black bear sleeping.

Then one day, they saw something very interesting. Whiteheart had woken up, but only for a short time. She stood and inspected the opening of her den, perhaps to see what the weather was like outside. Scientists think she might have wanted to go out for water, but because the snow was thick that day, she did not leave the den. Instead, she sniffed the camera, got comfortable again, and laid down. Soon Whiteheart was back in her hibernation sleep.

This might not seem like much, but scientists now had proof that hibernation was not one long, unbroken sleep, but sleep for weeks at a time with short bursts of activity.

## Spring Arrives

On March 31, Whiteheart woke up again. She stepped out of her den, felt the ice on the ground, and then went right back in. A late winter snap of cold kept her inside for a little while longer, but on April 9, Whiteheart left her den for good. Spring had come, and this black bear was ready to eat!

Unfortunately, Whiteheart slipped her radio collar off a few days later, and the scientists lost track of her. Now that it was spring, she had no further use of her winter den, so the scientists also shut down the Webcam. Even so, Whiteheart had still given them a lot of great information about how black bears survive the winter.

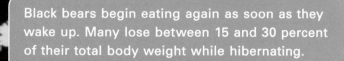

Black bears begin eating again as soon as they wake up. Many lose between 15 and 30 percent of their total body weight while hibernating.

# Torpor, the Light Sleepers

Whiteheart and other hibernators go into a deep sleep for long periods of time. But there are some animals that hibernate for only a very short time—sometimes just for a few hours.

This is called **torpor**. Torpor is like a mini-hibernation. When an animal is in torpor sleep, its metabolic rate slows down, its heart rate slows, and its body temperature drops, just like in hibernation. The animal will also curl up in a warm den or other shelter.

But instead of sleeping for weeks at a time, the animal will wake up the next morning. They stay awake during the day when they can hunt for food, but at night when the temperature drops, they go back into this mini-hibernation. Torpor sleep is much deeper than the animal's regular sleep. It has to be if the animal is going to avoid **hypothermia** when its body temperature falls to half of what it normally is. Torpor helps animals like badgers, raccoons, chipmunks, and wild hamsters survive the coldest parts of the winter while still letting them hunt for food.

Animals like badgers, foxes, and weasels brave the winter snows during the day when it's warmer and food is easier to find.

The hummingbird is one of the few species of birds to use torpor sleep. A hummingbird usually eats about twice its body weight every day. During the winter months, however, this much food is hard to find. And so, the hummingbird goes into a state of torpor so its body needs less food to live.

During the night when it's too cold to search for food, the hummingbird enters a sleep that's so deep it looks as though the bird might be dead. In 1832, an **ornithologist** named Alexander Wilson first observed torpor in hummingbirds. He said, "No motion of the lungs could be seen . . . the eyes were shut, and, when touched by the finger, it gave no signs of life."

It usually takes about 20 minutes or more for an animal to wake up from torpor. The temperature of its body slowly rises, its heart rate increases, and its metabolic rate returns to normal. By the time morning arrives, the animal is up and ready to spend the chilly day searching for food.

So why don't these animals hibernate instead of going into a torpor sleep? Because their bodies are so small, they aren't able to store enough fat to live on for more than one night. Hibernators like the black bear are huge. They're able to pack on enough fat to live for weeks and months. Torpor animals sleep a lot to save energy, but they also have to eat as much as they can every day.

Small animals have small bodies, so they aren't able to store much body fat. Unlike the black bear who can store fat for the whole winter, some animals use torpor to save energy between daily meals.

# Hibernation vs. Torpor

Hibernation and torpor are two very useful survival strategies for making it through the winter. They're both alike in many ways—if you can't stand the cold, find a cozy spot and sleep through it. But they're also quite different. How do hibernation and torpor compare to one another?

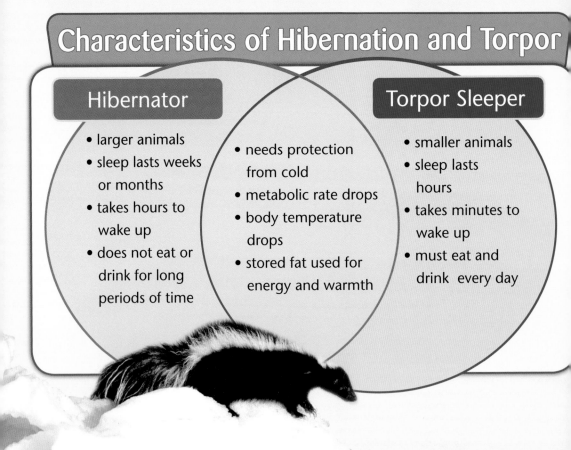

## Characteristics of Hibernation and Torpor

### Hibernator

- larger animals
- sleep lasts weeks or months
- takes hours to wake up
- does not eat or drink for long periods of time

- needs protection from cold
- metabolic rate drops
- body temperature drops
- stored fat used for energy and warmth

### Torpor Sleeper

- smaller animals
- sleep lasts hours
- takes minutes to wake up
- must eat and drink every day

## What Is It?

| What Is It? | Hibernation | Torpor |
|---|---|---|
| A very deep sleep that looks like the animal might be dead | ✓ | ✓ |
| Sleep that last for weeks or months | ✓ | |
| Sleep that lasts for hours or overnight | | ✓ |
| It takes a few hours to wake up | ✓ | |
| It takes 20 minutes or more to wake up | | ✓ |

## What Happens?

| What Happens? | Hibernation | Torpor |
|---|---|---|
| Metabolic rate drops | ✓ | ✓ |
| Body temperature drops 10% to 50% | ✓ | |
| Body temperature drops 50% or more | | ✓ |
| Stored fat is used for energy and warmth | ✓ | ✓ |

## Who Does It?

| Who Does It? | Hibernation | Torpor |
|---|---|---|
| Animals that need protection from cold | ✓ | ✓ |
| Usually large animals | ✓ | |
| Usually small animals | | ✓ |

# Chapter Two

# Migration Vacation

Sleeping the winter away may work for some animals, but others would rather take a vacation to a warmer climate. These creatures **migrate** when winter comes, traveling to places that are warmer and where food is easier to find.

In the fall, you can often see V-shaped flocks of birds flying south for the winter. They're not the only ones on the move. Birds and butterflies, whales and caribou, and even earthworms migrate.

They all go in search of warmer weather, but many are traveling to parts of the globe they've never been before. How do they know where they're going?

For the most part, animals migrate on **instinct**. Instinct is something an animal is born with; it is not taught. Instinct tells an animal to behave or do something in a certain way. For example, if there's a fire in a forest, even the youngest deer knows to stay away. It wasn't taught that fire is dangerous; it simply knows it by instinct.

Instinct plays a big part in when, how, and where animals migrate. Birds, such as the Arctic tern, travel great distances on difficult journeys. Other creatures, such as the earthworm, don't go very far at all.

# Flying South for the Winter

About 5 billion birds from 500 different species leave their summer homes and nesting grounds each year to spend the winter months further south. Most birds from the United States end up in Mexico, Central and South America, and the Caribbean Islands.

The Arctic tern migrates the longest distance of any animal. It leaves its home at the North Pole each fall and flies all the way to the South Pole, then returns again in the spring. That's more than 21,750 miles each year—roughly the entire distance around the earth.

Many birds travel at night and spend their days feeding and resting. But there are some daytime flyers, too. These birds, such as swallows and purple martins, can capture insects and eat them in midair.

During their lifetimes, most Arctic terns will fly over 400,000 miles—that's the distance from the earth to the moon and back!

Some birds do not land at all during their journey—not even to eat or rest. While other types of hummingbirds use torpor sleep to survive the winter, ruby-throated hummingbirds migrate south. This hummingbird travels nonstop across the Gulf of Mexico. That's nearly 500 miles without stopping! This means that they really have to eat a lot before taking off. The ruby-throated hummingbird will double its weight before the trip, then burn it all and more during the flight.

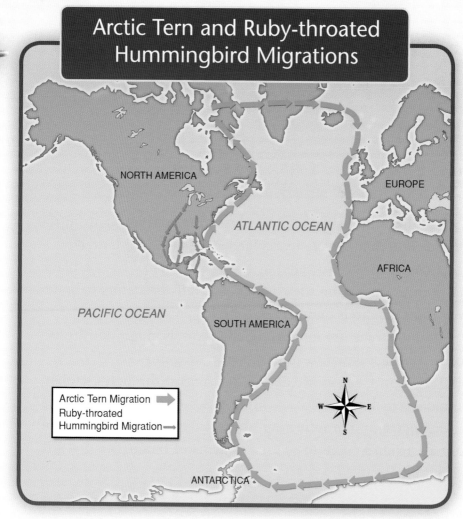

## Arctic Tern and Ruby-throated Hummingbird Migrations

NORTH AMERICA

EUROPE

ATLANTIC OCEAN

AFRICA

PACIFIC OCEAN

SOUTH AMERICA

Arctic Tern Migration
Ruby-throated
Hummingbird Migration

ANTARCTICA

## The Monarch Migration

In addition to birds, many insects also migrate south in the fall. But no other insects fly as far as the monarch butterfly. Monarchs are well protected as they travel. They have a black and orange pattern on their wings that tells predators to stay away. The monarch butterfly is actually poisonous!

The monarchs are famous for their yearly migration from North America down to Angangueo (ahn-gahn-GWAY-o), a small town in Central Mexico. From August through October, the monarchs fly as much as 3,000 miles to their winter home in Angangeuo, often returning to the exact same trees. People from all around come to see the swarms of butterflies that fill the sky like smoke.

## Monarch Butterfly Migrations

CANADA

UNITED STATES

GULF OF MEXICO

N
W E
S

MEXICO

Fall Migration →

Why the monarchs have chosen Angangeuo is a mystery, but an even bigger mystery is how they find their way back there every year. Individual butterflies only make the journey once because monarch adults only live for about six weeks. This means that it's their children's grandchildren that return south the following fall. After three generations have passed, how do the monarchs know where to go? Scientists believe that instinct plays a part in leading the monarchs to Angangeuo, just like instinct guides all migrating animals.

## The Long Walk

Not all animals that migrate move through the air, however. Both land animals and **marine** animals also migrate when the weather turns chilly.

Huge herds of caribou (also known as reindeer) travel south from their homes in Alaska and northern Canada every year. They not only hope to escape below-freezing temperatures, caribou must also migrate in search of food. The plants and grass that the caribou eat cannot survive in very cold temperatures. They go **dormant** during the winter, meaning they stop growing for a time. And so, the caribou must travel south to climates that still have plenty of plants to eat.

Caribou keep walking until spring, when it's time to turn right back around and head north again. Once they get back to their northern homes, it's fall once more—time to migrate south! Caribou are always on the move. Throughout the year a herd might walk over 2,500 miles.

Luckily these animals were built for walking. Their wide hooves work like snowshoes, helping them step through snow and ice. These wide hooves also help them swim. Despite their size, caribou are surprisingly good swimmers. If they come upon a stream or river in their path, they won't hesitate to dive right in and swim across.

The caribou's hooves are perfectly designed for snow and water. They're extra-wide, making them excellent snowshoes and paddles!

## Caribou Migration

BEAUFORT SEA

BERING SEA

ALASKA

CANADA

N
W — E
S

Fall Migration
Spring Migration

PACIFIC OCEAN

## Through Icy Waters

Each year, humpback whales leave the cold waters off the coasts of Maine and Massachusetts and head south for the warm waters of the Caribbean Sea.

During the fall, Arctic winds from the north begin making the ocean waters very cold. Humpback whales cannot give birth to their offspring, called calves, in such cold waters. So, the herd swims south all along the eastern coast of the United States to their **breeding grounds** just north of the Dominican Republic.

The trip is about 3,100 miles, and it takes the herd from 6 to 8 weeks to complete. The humpback mothers must hurry to make it to the breeding grounds before it's time to give birth, so the herd rests very little along the way.

The humpback whale can actually sing! The song of the humpback is the exact same song in every herd, sung over and over again as they migrate.

In the spring after the herd's calves are born, the humpbacks migrate north again to the cooler waters, where they feed. Humpback adults do not eat during the winter months. Instead, they live on a thick layer of fat. It's only during the summer months in the north that humpbacks eat enough to replace the fat they've lived on during the past winter.

Humpback Whale Migration

ATLANTIC OCEAN

Bahamas

Cuba

Puerto Rico

Haiti  Dominican Republic

Fall Migration
Spring Migration

# The Earth Moves

While many animals make long and incredible journeys, there are some who don't have to migrate very far at all. A short trip is just enough for the earthworm.

The ground during the winter will often freeze solid with ice. Freezing will kill the earthworm, so it migrates about six feet straight down into the soil. There it digs a cozy hole where it will wait until the ground thaws.

Earthworms have the ability to regenerate, or regrow, parts that get cut off. If you cut off an earthworm's head, it will grow a new one!

An earthworm can't breathe if its skin dries out. So it coils up and covers the inside of its nest with a slimy **mucus** to keep moist. It will stay in this slime-covered ball all winter.

Unlike other creatures who often go hungry in the winter, there's always something for the earthworm to eat. Worms live on bacteria, **protozoa**, decayed plants, and other things that are so small you can only see them with a microscope. The autumn leaves that fall to the ground decay, giving the earthworm a feast all winter long.

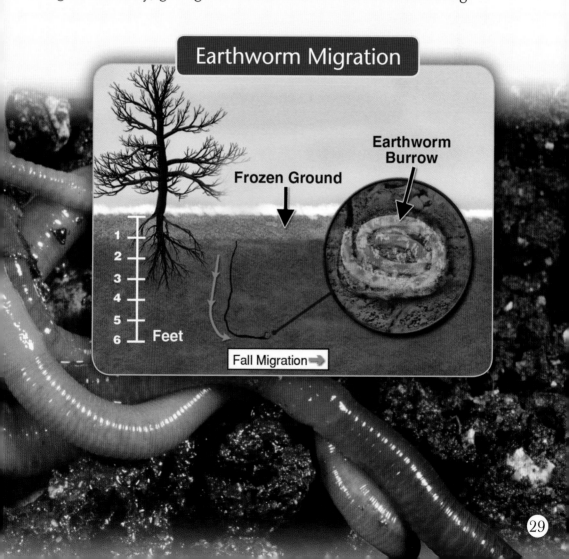

## Earthworm Migration

Earthworm Burrow

Frozen Ground

1
2
3
4
5
6
Feet

Fall Migration ➡

# By Air, Sea, or Land

When the weather turns cold, these migrating animals are on the move. Some have a long way to go and not a lot of time. For others, a cozy winter home is just a wiggle away.

What are the differences between migrating by air, sea, and land?

## How Far Do They Go?

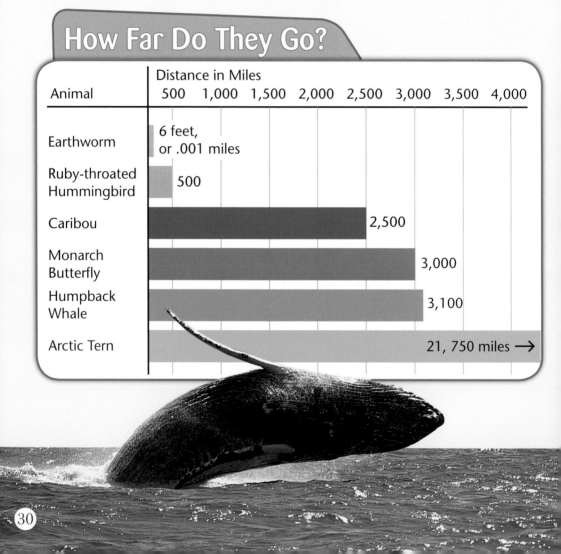

| Animal | Distance in Miles | | | | | | | |
|---|---|---|---|---|---|---|---|---|
| | 500 | 1,000 | 1,500 | 2,000 | 2,500 | 3,000 | 3,500 | 4,000 |
| Earthworm | 6 feet, or .001 miles | | | | | | | |
| Ruby-throated Hummingbird | 500 | | | | | | | |
| Caribou | | | | | 2,500 | | | |
| Monarch Butterfly | | | | | | 3,000 | | |
| Humpback Whale | | | | | | 3,100 | | |
| Arctic Tern | | | | | | | 21, 750 miles → | |

## Who Does It?

| Through the Air | Under the Sea | Across the Land |
|---|---|---|
| 500 species of birds | Marine life | Caribou |
| Monarch butterflies | Humpback whales | Earthworms |

## When Do They Go?

| Through the Air | Under the Sea | Across the Land |
|---|---|---|
| Late September through the fall | When the water gets chilly in late fall | Caribou walk nonstop all year |
| Monarch butterflies fly from August to October every year | Humpback whales return to the cool waters in the north every summer | Earthworms migrate just before the ground freezes |

## Where Are They Going?

| Through the Air | Under the Sea | Across the Land |
|---|---|---|
| Birds in North America fly south for the winter | Humpbacks go from the northeast corner of the U.S. down to the Caribbean Sea | Caribou walk south until spring |
| Monarchs travel south to Angangeuo in Central Mexico | Many marine animals travel to breeding grounds in warmer waters | Earthworms dig six feet straight down |

# Chapter Three

# Amazing Animal Adaptations

Some creatures don't hibernate or migrate. Instead, they stay home and try to keep warm during the winter. These animals need special tools to help them survive the cold temperatures and lack of food. These tools are called **physical adaptations**.

A physical adaptation can be something the animal has, such as thick fur or feathers, or it can be something an animal does, such as sleeping under the snow or sharing body heat. These adaptations develop slowly over long periods of time and over many generations, making the species stronger and better able to survive.

There is a wide range of different adaptations, some much stranger than others. Hair, fat, and feathers all play a role in keeping animals warm. But in some animals, you can also find such odd adaptations as snow diving, antifreeze in the blood, and **camouflage**. And what about the animal with the extra-bushy tail that works like an electric blanket? Or the one with not one fur coat, but two?

And so, straight from the case files of "Amazing Animal Adaptations" comes this odd **menagerie** of animals specially designed to not just survive, but thrive in the white world of winter.

**Name:** Musk Ox

**Scientific Name:** *Ovibos moschatus*

**Description:** A large, ox-like animal with thick
hair and a musky odor

**Location:** Northern Canada and Greenland

**Physical Adaptation:** Hairy beast of the north

The musk ox seems to be built almost entirely out of hair. The native Inuit people call this animal *umingmak*, meaning "animal with skin like a beard." All of this hair protects the musk ox from the biting cold and howling winds of winter in the far north.

The musk ox actually has two fur coats: a shaggy outer layer and a soft and woolly inner layer. The hair in the outer layer can be almost three feet long and reach all the way down to the ox's feet. The inner layer helps keep the ox's body heat from escaping. When the weather warms up, the musk ox sheds this undercoat.

**Name:** Emperor Penguin

**Scientific Name:** *Aptenodytes forsteri*

**Description:** One of the largest penguin species; known for yellow-orange patches on neck

**Location:** Antarctic regions of the South Pole

**Physical Adaptation:** Master of the huddle

Emperor penguins have four layers of scale-like feathers and a thick layer of body fat that keeps their bodies warm. The females lay the eggs, but the males are the ones who make sure they hatch.

The male penguin will balance his egg on top of his feet, then squat down so his body keeps the egg warm. Then, all the males will huddle close together. Huddling together like this helps share the warmth so none of the eggs get cold. Emperor penguins will spend over 65 days huddled together like this. What's more, they take turns in the warmest and coldest places in the huddle. These adaptations help emperor penguins survive temperatures of 28° F below zero.

**Name:** Polar Bear

**Scientific Name:** *Ursus maritimus*

**Description:** A huge bear with white fur

**Location:** Arctic regions of North America

**Physical Adaptation:** Hollow fur coat

The polar bear's fur coat is the perfect adaptation for surviving the snowy Arctic environment where it lives year-round. Each strand of fur is hollow, like a tiny little tube. These tube-like hairs trap the air that has been warmed by the bear's body so it doesn't escape.

These hollow hairs are also transparent, meaning they are colorless. Transparent fur allows sunlight to pass easily through, warming the bear's skin. Even though the polar bear looks white from a distance, it actually has black skin hidden beneath all that fur. Black is the color that absorbs heat the best, so having black skin helps keep the polar bear warm and toasty.

**Name:** Arctic Wolf
**Scientific Name:** *Canis lupus arctos*
**Description:** A large wolf with white fur
**Location:** Arctic regions of North America
**Physical Adaptation:** Camouflaged for hunting

The arctic wolf, also known as the white wolf, has thick, white fur that helps it blend in with the snow. In addition to providing warmth, the wolf's white coat is a useful camouflage. It helps the wolf sneak up on prey, which is very important because food for these meat-eaters is sometimes hard to come by in the arctic regions of the far north.

Also, the white camouflage helps the arctic wolf hide from other predators. Many scientists believe that the arctic wolf developed this adaptation after it had moved north to escape human hunters.

**Name:** Snowshoe Rabbit
**Scientific Name:** *Lepus americanus*
**Description:** A large hare, or rabbit, with large back feet and a white winter coat
**Location:** North America
**Physical Adaptation:** Color shifter

The snowshoe rabbit has brown fur in the summer, but when fall approaches, hairs with white tips start growing in. In about ten weeks, the snowshoe rabbit is solid white so it can blend in with the snow. White fur helps the rabbit hide from predators.

The snowshoe rabbit also grows long hairs between the toes of its back feet, which work like snowshoes to keep it from sinking into deep snow. You can often see lots of rabbit tracks in the woods during winter because rabbits spend their days out looking for food such as grass, buds, and the bark from bushes.

**Name:** Ruffed Grouse
**Scientific Name:** *Bonasa umbellus*
**Description:** A chicken-like bird with brown feathers
**Location:** North America
**Physical Adaptation:** Extreme snow diver

The ruffed grouse doesn't need to fly south for the winter. This bird is well-suited for the cold. It grows spines along the sides of its toes so it can travel easily over deep, soft snow.

When a snowstorm comes, the ruffed grouse will jump headfirst into a snow bank! It's warmer under the snow, so the grouse will remain there until the storm is over. Hiding in packed snow also protects this bird from predators. The ruffed grouse sleeps under the snow during the cold of night, and when morning comes, it comes out to eat buds, berries, and evergreen needles.

**Name:** The Gray Squirrel
**Scientific Name:** *Sciurus carolinensis*
**Description:** A common squirrel with gray or black fur
**Location:** Eastern parts of North America
**Physical Adaptation:** Nose for food finding

This little mammal knows how to prepare for a long winter. The gray squirrel busily collects acorns and nuts during the fall, burying each one individually. When winter comes, it uses its good memory and strong sense of smell to find these goodies, even if the food is buried deep in the snow. One squirrel can eat about forty pounds of acorns in a single winter!

As the cold approaches, the gray squirrel's coat grows thicker, and its bushy tail become even bushier. At night while it sleeps, the gray squirrel will keep warm by wrapping its furry tail around its face.

**Name:** Wood Frog
**Scientific Name:** *Rana sylvatic*
**Description:** A woodland frog with a brown patch
on its face
**Location:** North America
**Physical Adaptation:** The frozen frog

If you think you see a frozen frog in the woods in wintertime, don't worry. That "frogcicle" isn't dead. When winter's chill arrives, the wood frog hides under a pile of leaves. Then something odd happens. Ice crystals form inside the frog's body, causing it to stop breathing! Its heart stops beating! The wood frog doesn't freeze solid, though, since sugar in its blood acts like antifreeze in the creature's vital organs. Antifreeze is a chemical that makes it harder for a liquid to freeze. The woodland frog's natural antifreeze keeps its cells from freezing, even if the frog's body temperature falls below 0° F!

When the weather warms up, the frog thaws out and hops back into action. Some other North American frogs, such as spring peepers and chorus frogs, have this same adaptation.

# Animal Adaptations

There's a wide range of strange ways to survive the winter. Whether it's diving headfirst into the snow, growing out your fur coat, or just freezing yourself,
each of these animals has come up with its own survival strategy.

Such adaptations may seem a little unusual, but without them, these animals wouldn't be able to live in the ice and snow!

## Strange Ways to Keep Warm

| Animal | Adapation |
|---|---|
| Ruffled Grouse | Dives headfirst into the snow |
| Emperor Penguins | Eggs balanced on top of its feet, the penguins huddle close together for warmth |
| Wood Frog | Sugars in the blood act like an antifreeze |

## Camouflage

| Animal | Adapation |
|--------|-----------|
| Arctic Wolf | Solid-white fur lets it hide as it hunts prey |
| Snowshoe Rabbit | Solid-white fur lets it hide from its predators |

## Unusual Fur Coats

| Animal | Adapation |
|--------|-----------|
| Musk Ox | Has not one, but two fur coats |
| Grey Squirrel | Super-bushy tail it wraps around itself |
| Emperor Penguin | Has four layers of scale-like feathers |
| Polar Bear | Transparent, hollow hair and black skin that heats up in the sun |

## Finding Food

| Animal | Adapation |
|--------|-----------|
| Grey Squirrel | Hides acorns in the fall to eat during winter |
| Ruffled Grouse | Hides under snow all night, then comes out during the day to hunt for food |

# Super Winter Survivor

Now that you've read the case files, it's time to think about putting these survival strategies into action.

Pretend it's your job to put together a winter animal using the different strategies discussed in this book. Which do you think work best? Which will help your survivor make it through to spring? Remember, your animal will need to be able to survive freezing temperatures, cold winds, and months with very little food.

Give your animal a name, then imagine it overcoming the cold as a Super Winter Survivor!

### Hibernation
Find a cozy den and sleep the winter away.

### Torpor
Escape the freezing temperatures at night with this mini-hibernation.

### Migration
Get out of town! Fly, swim, or walk south for the winter.

## Winter Instincts

The cold is coming, but where will you go? Use your instincts to find a warm place to spend the winter.

## Camouflage for Protection

Change your fur solid white to hide from predators.

## Extra Fur

Stay warm by growing a think winter coat.

## Extra Fat

Eat as much as you can in the fall to pack on a thick layer of fat to keep you warm.

## Camouflage for Hunting

Change your fur solid white to help hunt for prey.

## Antifreeze in the Blood

Keep yourself from freezing solid with these special sugars in the bloodstream.

## Snow Diving

Escape the cold by sleeping under the snow.

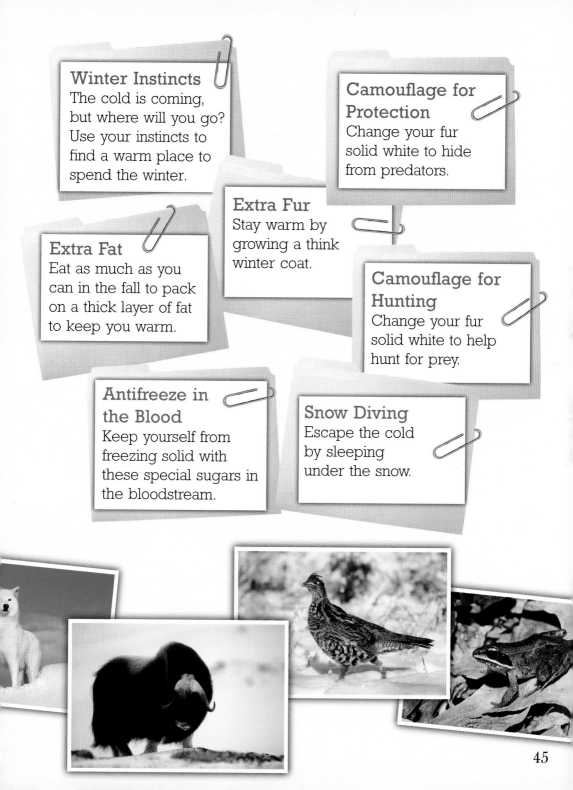

# Glossary

**adapt** to make yourself ready for a certain situation or environment

**breeding grounds** a place where animals go every year to give birth or lay eggs

**camouflage** a disguise or change in skin or fur color that helps the animal blend into its environment so that it can't be seen

**dormant** to be asleep or not moving

**hibernation** a deep sleep in which some animals spend all or part of the winter

**hypothermia** when the body's temperature falls dangerously low

**instinct** a type of behavior or knowledge that an animal is born with and does not have to be taught

**marine** having to do with the ocean or the animals that live in the ocean

**menagerie** a collection of live, wild animals

**metabolic rate** a measure of how much energy that an animal uses to live

**migrate** to move from one place to another

**mucus** a slick, slippery substance produce by the body

**ornithologist** a scientist who studies birds

**pelt** an animal's fur

**physical adaptation** a change in an animal's body or appearance that helps it prepare for a certain situation or environment

**protozoa** a microscopic organism that is made of only one cell

**survival strategy** a plan of action used to help an animal live through a difficult time

**torpor** a deep sleep in which some animals spend only a few hours or overnight

**transparent** see-through; invisible

# Index